Peacocks

by Ruth Berman
photographs by Richard R. Hewett

Lerner Publications Company • Minneapolis, Minnesota

To Robbie and Kurt
        —RB

To Joan, Angela, and Chris
        —RRH

The photographer would like to thank the California Arboretum Foundation, Arboretum of L.A. County; and Don Jim

Thanks to our series consultant, Sharyn Fenwick, elementary science/math specialist. Mrs. Fenwick was the winner of the National Science Teachers Association 1991 Distinguished Teaching Award. She also was the recipient of the Presidential Award for Excellence in Math and Science Teaching, representing the state of Minnesota at the elementary level in 1992. And special thanks to our young helper, Ben Liestman.

Ruth Berman, series editor
Steve Foley, series designer

Library of Congress Cataloging-in-Publication Data

Berman, Ruth.
    Peacocks / Ruth Berman ; photographs by Richard R. Hewett.
        p. cm. — (Early bird nature books)
    Includes index.
    ISBN 0-8225-3009-0
    1. Peafowl — Juvenile literature. [1. Peacocks.] I. Hewett,
Richard, ill. II. Title. III. Series.
QL696.G27B47 1996
598.6'17 — dc20 95-12204

Manufactured in the United States of America
1 2 3 4 5 6 – SP – 01 00 99 98 97 96

Contents

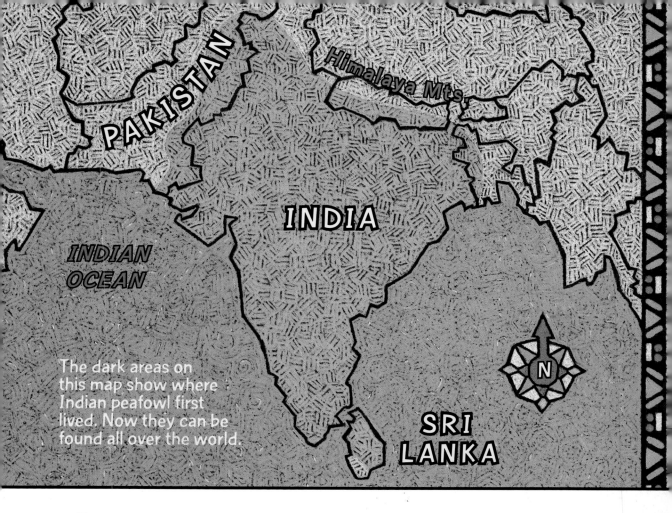

The dark areas on this map show where Indian peafowl first lived. Now they can be found all over the world.

Be a Word Detective

Can you find these words as you read about the peacock's life? Be a detective and try to figure out what they mean. You can turn to the glossary on page 46 for help.

clutch   harem   polygamous

crest   incubate   preen

crop   molting   spur

display   omnivores

Chapter 1

Adult peacocks have longer and more colorful feathers than adult peahens. What do peacocks and peahens have that are the same?

Blue Beauties

The peacock is one of the most beautiful birds in the world. You've probably seen one at a zoo. Chances are you've seen a peahen too. But you probably didn't pay much attention to her. Peahens don't have the long, colorful feathers that peacocks have. Both peacocks and peahens have crests, though. A crest is a crown of feathers on a bird's head. Peacocks are males. Peahens are females. The babies are called peachicks. Altogether, these birds are called peafowl.

Both a peacock (top) *and a peahen* (bottom) *grow a crest of feathers on their heads.*

Peacocks have blue necks and peahens have green necks. The peacocks on the rail are too young to have their long, colorful feathers.

Peafowl are polygamous (peh-LIH-geh-muss). A polygamous family is made up of one adult male and many adult females. One peacock and four to six peahens make up a peafowl family. The group of peahens in a family is called a harem (HAIR-ehm).

Peafowl are related to chickens. They're really a type of pheasant (FEH-zuhnt), though. All pheasants have long, colorful feathers. And all pheasants have long, scaly bare legs.

A peacock weighs about 10 pounds. He can be 6–8 feet long, including 4-6 feet of colorful feathers.

Three species, or kinds, of peafowl live in the world. They are the Congo, the green, and the Indian peafowl. Indian peafowl are also called blue or common peafowl. They are the ones we see most often at zoos. And this is their story.

The scientific name of the Indian peafowl is Pavo cristatus.

Chapter 2

Peafowl live in places like India where it is hot. Can they live in cold places too?

Indian Peafowl

Peafowl have been living in India for over 50,000 years. India can be very hot. But peafowl don't mind the heat. They can live through frosty cold weather too. So peafowl can live almost anywhere.

Wild peafowl live in grassy parklike areas. Peafowl in zoos spend time in grassy areas too.

Over thousands of years, people have brought peafowl to live all over the world. Now peafowl live in zoos and parks. Some even live in people's backyards.

In India, peafowl live in open areas like parks. The land is grassy. A few trees and shrubs grow here and there. Open areas make it easy for peafowl to look out for enemies. Sometimes peafowl look out for enemies while roosting in trees.

Peafowl can hear and see very well. This peacock searches for enemies while he roosts high in a tree.

When peafowl roost, they sit on branches high up in a tree. They feel safest in a tree that stands alone. That way they can see all around them. At night, peafowl sleep while roosting with their families. They are hidden in the tree. They are safe from their enemies.

Enemies would have a hard time seeing this roosting peacock.

The tiger is one of the peafowl's enemies.

Peafowl listen and look for enemies. Tigers, leopards, and jackals are predators. They hunt and eat other animals. To get away from these predators, peafowl fly into trees. Hawk-eagles are predators too. They are birds of prey. Peafowl are prey. Prey are the animals predators eat. Peafowl run under bushes to get away from birds of prey.

Chapter 3

Peafowl don't fly very often. Peacocks don't fly as well as peahens because a peacock's long feathers are heavy. Will this peacock land smoothly?

Nibbling and Gobbling

It's morning. Everything is still and quiet. The sun isn't up yet. A family of birds flies out of a tall tree. The leader is a peacock. The birds following him are all peahens. They swoop to the ground, making a clumsy landing.

The peacock leads his harem to food and water. In the wild, peafowl eat and drink in the morning and in the afternoon. But in captivity, in zoos and parks, peafowl nibble all day long.

Peafowl find most of their food on the ground. Sometimes they chase and eat butterflies and other insects.

Peafowl are omnivores (AHM-nih-vorz). They eat almost anything they find. They eat grains like wheat, corn, and rice. They eat flowers. Sometimes, they eat other animals. In India, they even eat cobras!

Peafowl eat almost anything they find. This peacock is eating a flower.

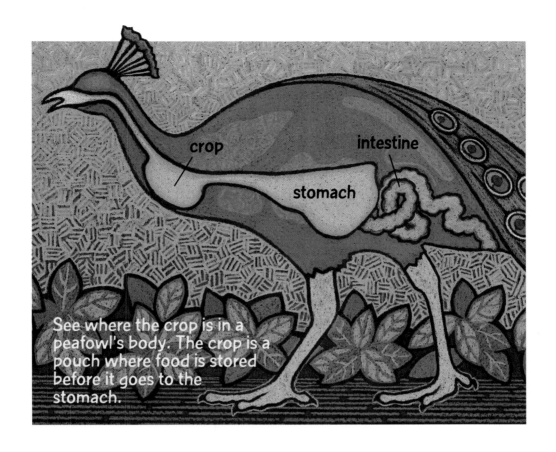

See where the crop is in a peafowl's body. The crop is a pouch where food is stored before it goes to the stomach.

Peafowl do not have teeth. Instead, they gobble up whole pieces of food. The food is stored in their bodies. It is stored in a pouch called the crop. Food from the crop goes into the stomach. Sometimes, peafowl swallow sand and small rocks. But this doesn't hurt them. Sand and rocks help a bird's stomach crush food.

Chapter 4

A peacock's colorful feathers are just decoration. Other feathers keep peafowl warm. How do peafowl stay cool?

A Fan of Feathers

Feathers help peafowl stay warm in cold weather. Feathers help peafowl stay cool in hot weather too. When it's cold, peafowl fluff up their feathers. Fluffy feathers have many air spaces. Heat from a peafowl's body is trapped in the fluffy feathers. So the bird stays warm.

Heat is flowing out of this peacock's open mouth.

When it's hot, peafowl don't fluff up their feathers. Instead, they press their feathers close to their bodies. Now body heat can escape, and the peafowl stay cool. Sometimes, peafowl keep their mouths wide open. That's because body heat flows out of a peafowl's mouth too.

Peafowl, like other birds, have three types of feathers. They are flight feathers, contour (KAHN-toor) feathers, and down. Peafowl have flight feathers on their wings and tails. These are straight and stiff feathers that help birds fly.

Peafowl have three types of feathers. The brown wings are made of flight feathers. The white-and-black striped feathers are contour feathers. And the fuzzy feathers are down.

This peacock is beginning to show off his colorful feathers. These feathers are a special kind of contour feather.

Contour feathers cover a peafowl's body. They make a bird look smooth. Under the contour feathers are small, fuzzy down feathers. Down is also the first kind of feather that grows on peachicks. All feathers are made of layers of keratin (KEHR-uh-tihn). Your skin, hair, and fingernails are made of keratin too.

Of course, the most beautiful feathers are the peacock's train. The train is made up of 150-200 feathers. Each train feather is from 3 to 6 feet long. At the end of each feather is a spot. The spot looks like an eye. Most people even call it the eyespot. But scientists call it the ocellus. Many eyespots are called ocelli. In the Latin language, *ocelli* means "little eyes." Since

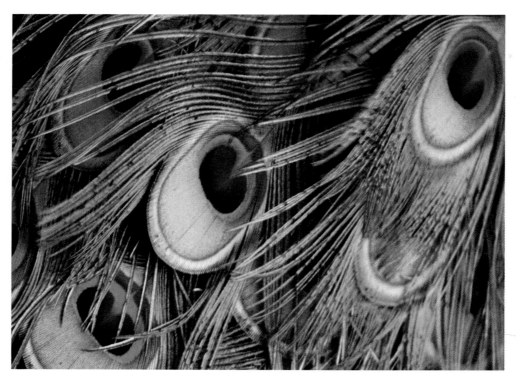

The ocelli, or eyespots, are at the end of each feather.

A peacock's train looks colorful because light hits it from many different directions.

each feather is a different length, the eyespots look like they are sprinkled all over the train.

The peacock's train looks bright. It looks like it is full of many different colors. But the train feathers are really just brown. Light hits the feathers from different directions and makes the feathers look colorful.

In this back-end view, you can see the peacock's tail holding up his train.

The train is not the peafowl's tail. The tail is under the train. And the tail is made of 20 light brown feathers. A peacock often spreads his train up into a fan. This is called the

When a peacock displays, his fan can be 9 feet wide.

display. Sometimes a peacock displays for only a few seconds. But sometimes he displays for over an hour. When a peacock displays, his tail helps hold up his train.

A peacock beats his wings and shakes to spread his train into a fan.

During a display, muscles on a peacock's rump lift up his tail feathers. The train is forced upward too. The peacock beats his wings and shakes. The train spreads into a fan. The peacock starts strutting around like he's

28

dancing. Some people think he has to strut to keep his balance. Strutting is important if strong winds are blowing. The wind might catch in a peacock's fan and knock him over!

A peacock displays for a peahen. His fan makes a soft rattling sound as he shakes it.

A peacock has many reasons to display. He displays to dazzle peahens. He displays when he sees his own reflection. Sometimes he displays just because he feels like it. And a peacock displays before fighting with another peacock. Peacocks can't see behind them when they are displaying. So a peacock displaying before a fight has to be careful. His enemy might peck him on the rump!

A peacock calls when he displays, when enemies are near, and when he's about to roost. His call can be heard up to 2 miles away.

Peacocks fight each other with their feet and spurs.

Peacocks use their legs to fight with each other. They have a sharp spur on each leg. They attack with their spurs. Peacocks fight each other to get peahens to join their harems. And they fight to protect their home areas.

Chapter 5

This peahen preens to keep her feathers neat and clean. How does oil help keep her dry?

Neat and Clean

Peafowl take care of their feathers by preening. All birds preen. They use their beaks to smooth their feathers. They use their beaks to spread oil through their feathers too.

A peafowl's body makes oil right near the front of the tail. Oil keeps water off a peafowl. Oil and water don't mix. So water slips off the oily feathers. Peafowl often preen while they are roosting.

A peacock spreads oil through his feathers.

Sometimes peafowl get too oily when they preen. Dust soaks up extra oil. So peafowl take dust baths. First, they scrape up dirt. Then they lie on the ground. They flap their wings to toss dust over themselves. Then they stand up, shake themselves off, and preen some more.

Peafowl take dust baths when they've become too oily.

A peacock is in the process of molting.

Once every summer, a peafowl's feathers fall off. Old feathers fall off so new feathers can grow in. This is called molting. Molting lasts a few weeks. But it takes about seven months for the new train feathers to grow back. Peafowl can still fly while they are molting, though. That's because the flight feathers are replaced quickly.

Chapter 6

This peachick is just a couple of weeks old. What kind of nest was it in when it hatched?

Eggs and Chicks

Peahens get ready to lay eggs in early summer. But they don't go to the trouble of building nests. They just find places under shrubs or in tall grass. Then they scrape away some of the dirt. That's a nest.

Sometimes, a peahen doesn't even lay her eggs in a nest. She lays them all around on the ground. She lays them in the same area, though. Then she gathers them into her nest.

Peahens scratch at the ground to make their nests.
They also scratch at the ground to find food.

Each of the six eggs in this clutch is about 3 inches long.

A peahen spends around a week laying her eggs. She lays about five to eight eggs. A group of eggs is called a clutch. A peahen can lay many clutches in a year. But her first clutch of the summer has the most eggs. After all her eggs are laid, the peahen is ready to incubate (ING-kyoo-bait) them.

Peahens incubate their eggs for 28 days.

The peahen has to make sure her chicks will develop and hatch. So she incubates her eggs by sitting on them. Incubation keeps eggs at the right temperature. The peahen incubates her eggs for 28 days. Sometimes many peahens lay their eggs together. Then they take turns incubating all the eggs.

When they hatch, peachicks are covered with feathers, and they can scramble away from the nest.

Peachicks spend many hours hatching out of their eggs. Each peachick has an egg tooth. The egg tooth is a hard point at the top of the beak. It is used to break through the eggshell. After a peachick has hatched, the egg tooth falls off.

When peachicks hatch, their eyes are open. They are covered with down feathers. And they can run around. Their flight feathers have already begun to grow. Peachicks begin to fly when they are one week old. Two-week-old peachicks can fly up to branches that are 3 feet off the ground. One-month-old peachicks have most of their adult feathers. Their crests have grown in too. But it takes up to six years for a peacock's train to grow to its full length.

The crest is just beginning to grow on this young peachick.

Peachicks stay with their families for up to nine weeks. Then they go off on their own. Soon, they will start new families.

Male and female peachicks under one year old look alike.

Peahens start their families when they are one year old. But peacocks are at least three years old before they start families.

The next time you go to a zoo, keep your eye out for peacocks. Are they molting or displaying? Are peahens nearby? What about peachicks? Are any of them roosting or preening? And remember, peafowl might be in your city zoo, but they first lived in a faraway land called India.

On Sharing a Book

As you know, adults greatly influence a child's attitude toward reading. When a child sees you read, or when you share a book with a child, you're sending a message that reading is important. Show your child that reading a book together is important to you. Find a comfortable, quiet place. Turn off the television and limit other distractions like telephone calls.

Be prepared to start slowly. Take turns reading parts of this book. Stop and talk about what you're reading. Talk about the photographs. You may find that much of the shared time is spent discussing just a few pages. This discussion time is valuable for both of you, so don't move through the book too quickly. If your child begins to lose interest, stop reading. Continue sharing the book at another time. When you do pick up the book again, be sure to revisit the parts you have already read. Most importantly, enjoy the book!

Be a Vocabulary Detective

You will find a word list on page 5. Words selected for this list are important to the understanding of the topic of this book. Encourage your child to be a word detective and search for the words as you read the book together. Talk about what the words mean and how they are used in the sentence. Do any of these words have more than one meaning? You will find these words defined in a glossary on page 46.

What about Questions?

Use questions to make sure your child understands the information in this book. Here are some suggestions:

> What did this paragraph tell us? What does this picture show? What do you think we'll learn about next? How are peafowl different from other birds you see every day? How are they the same? Do peafowl eat food the same way you do? If you had feathers, how would you stay warm if the weather were cold? How would you stay cool if the weather were hot? Why does a peacock strut? What is your favorite part of the book? Why?

If your child has questions, don't hesitate to respond with questions of your own like: What do *you* think? Why? What is it that you don't know? If your child can't remember certain facts, turn to the index.

44

Introducing the Index

The index is an important learning tool. It helps readers get information quickly without searching throughout the whole book. Turn to the index on page 47. Choose an entry such as *train,* and ask your child to use the index to find out how many feathers are in a peacock's train. Repeat this exercise with as many entries as you like. Ask your child to point out the differences between an index and a glossary. (The glossary tells readers what words mean, while the index helps readers find information quickly.)

All the World in Metric

Although our monetary system is in metric units (based on multiples of 10), the United States is one of the few countries in the world that does not use the metric system of measurement. Here are some conversion activities you and your child can do using a calculator:

WHEN YOU KNOW:	MULTIPLY BY:	TO FIND:
miles	1.609	kilometers
feet	0.3048	meters
inches	2.54	centimeters
gallons	3.787	liters
tons	0.907	metric tons
pounds	0.454	kilograms

Family Activities

Blow bubbles. Even though bubbles are clear, light shines on them and creates a rainbow of colors. What colors do you see? Are they the same colors you see on a peacock's train?

Pour a little cooking oil in a baking pan and rub it around with a paper towel. Drop some water in the pan and watch what happens. What does the water do? Pour the water into the sink. Is the pan still wet? Because they're oily, a peafowl's feathers respond to water in a similar way.

Visit a zoo and compare peafowl to the other birds that are there. Look at their feathers, feet, and beaks. What differences do you see? Do the variations help each type of bird live in its particular environment? How are all the birds similar?

Glossary

clutch—a nest of eggs

crest—a crown of feathers on a bird's head

crop—a pouch in a bird's body that stores food

display—the spreading of a peacock's long, colorful feathers into a fan

harem (HAIR-ehm)—the group of peahens in a peafowl family

incubate (ING-kyoo-bait)—to sit on eggs and keep them warm so they'll hatch

molting—the falling off of feathers so new ones can grow in

omnivores (AHM-nih-vorz)—animals who eat both plants and animals

polygamous (peh-LIH-geh-muss)—having one peacock and more than one peahen in the family

preen—to smooth feathers with a beak

spur—a sharp growth on a peacock's leg used for fighting

Index

Pages listed in **bold** type refer to photographs.

REBECCA KROENING

About the Author

Ruth Berman has been interested in the natural world since she was very young. She earned a B.A. in English from the University of Minnesota and turned her love for animals into a career. She has worked for the Sierra Club and for the Zoological Society of Philadelphia. Ruth currently edits science books for children. Her first book, Carolrhoda's *American Bison,* was chosen as an Outstanding Science Trade Book for Children.

DON JIM

About the Photographer

Richard R. Hewett was born and raised in St. Paul, Minnesota. He graduated from California's Art Center School of Design with a major in photo-journalism. For a number of years he freelanced for national magazines. Then he discovered children's books. Dick and his wife, writer Joan Hewett, live in southern California. *Peacocks* is his sixth book with the Lerner Group.

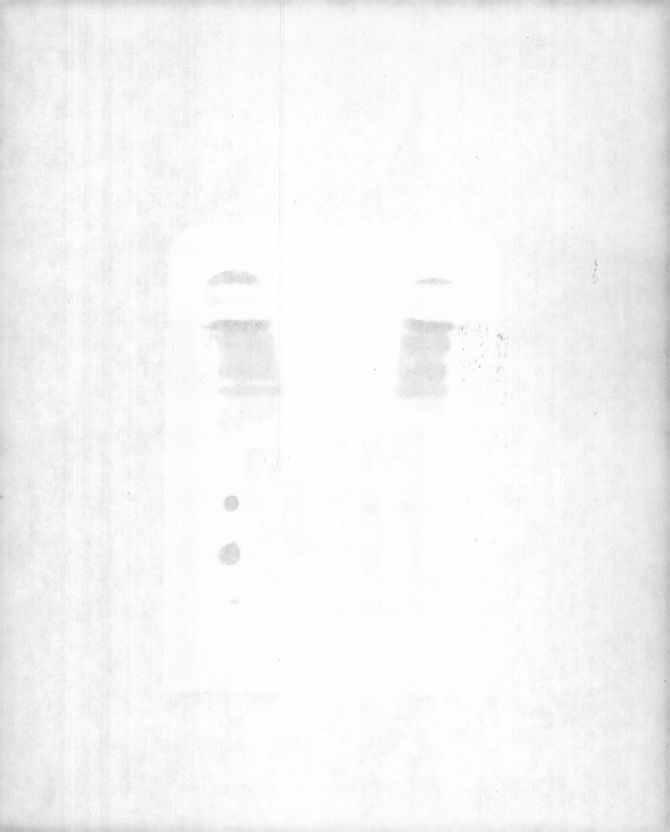